An Artistic Journey: A Young Adult Coloring Book Volume I

An Artistic Journey: A Young Adult Coloring Book Volume I

Developed by

Gary R. Brown

PLEASELETTHEMKNOW

The content of this book, **An Artistic Journey: A Young Adult Coloring Book Volume I** is copyrighted by **PleaseLetThemKnow, L.L.C**. for 2024. This content is protected by copyright law. You must first get written permission from the copyright owner before reproducing or distributing any part of it. Using or distributing this content without proper authorization may lead to legal consequences. Respect the owner's rights by doing the right thing. It's essential to consider the owner's rights both legally and morally. Please cooperate by honoring the owner's rights.

Gary R. Brown

Dedication

An Artistic Journey: A Young Adult Coloring Book Volume I is dedicated to my beloved grandson, Anthony Michael Harrell. Anthony Michael has always been a great source of motivation, and his words of inducement have helped me explore the world of activity books for children and adults. Whenever we are together with my daughter, we always have fun and play around, which inspired me to create this project and others that combine entertainment and education. Through this project, I have been able to delve deeper into the areas that young people are interested in and learn how to engage them in a fun and respectful way.

Unlike in my day when there were no computers or social media, kids today face different challenges, and it's crucial to help them stay grounded while having fun. In many ways, I wish we could return to those simpler times, but the present has its merits. Anthony, thank you for being my stimulation, and I hope these books will bring joy and learning to the minds of many young adults.

Table of Contents

Dedication..5
An Artistic Journey: A Young Adult Coloring Book Volume I Introduction..7
Coloring Book Pages..8-109
About the Developer..110-111

An Artistic Journey: A Young Adult Coloring Book Volume I

    I love to create books that both adults and children can enjoy. My books are designed to provide a fun and creative way to pass the time. I attend vendor events to showcase my new books, sell some copies, and give away others. My coloring books cover various styles, including primary and mandala, and feature exciting places to visit. I also plan to create books on fashion, anime, cartoons, and other popular topics. I hope you enjoy my latest book, Artful Adventures: A Young Adult Coloring Book Volume I, specifically designed for young adults.

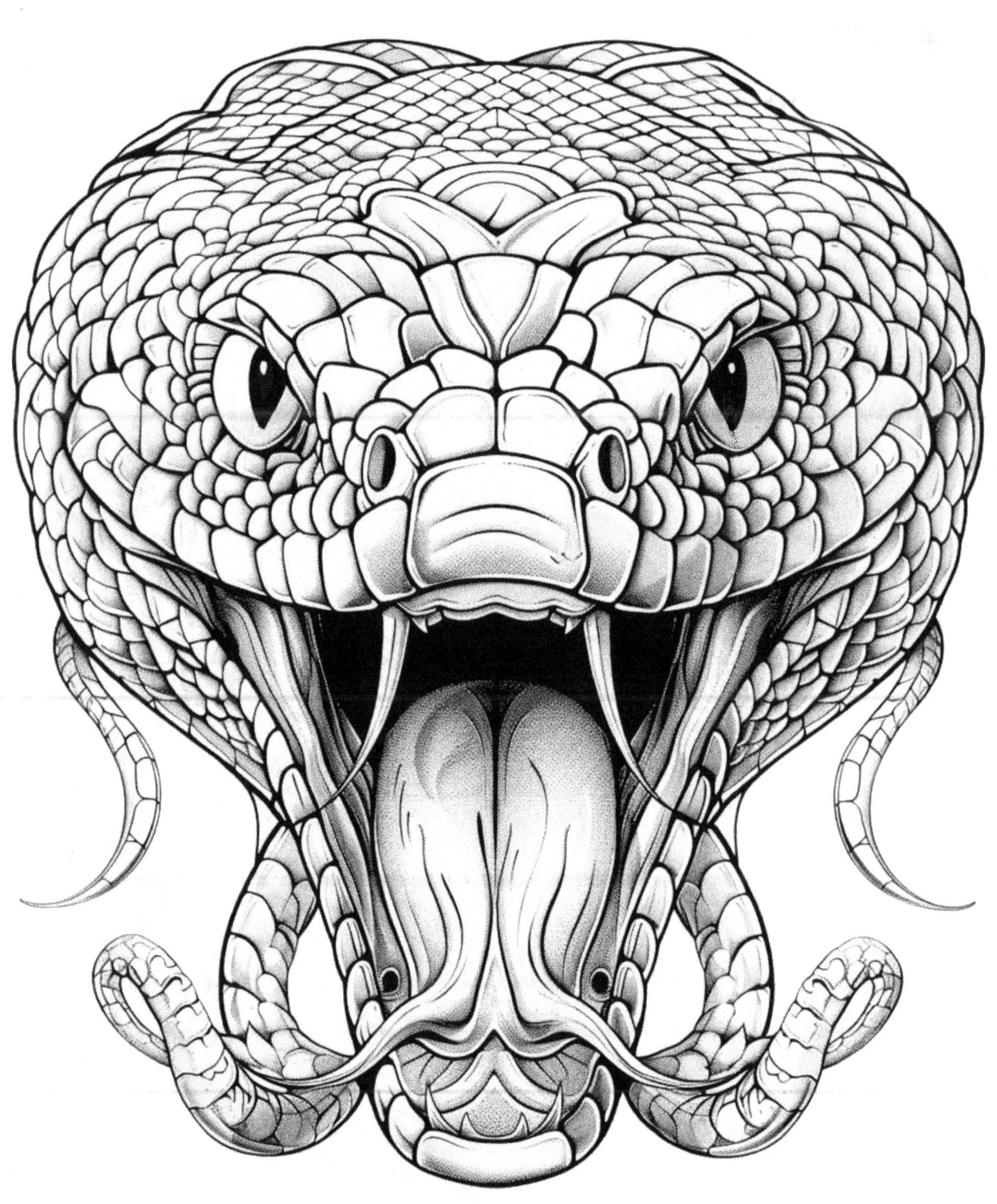

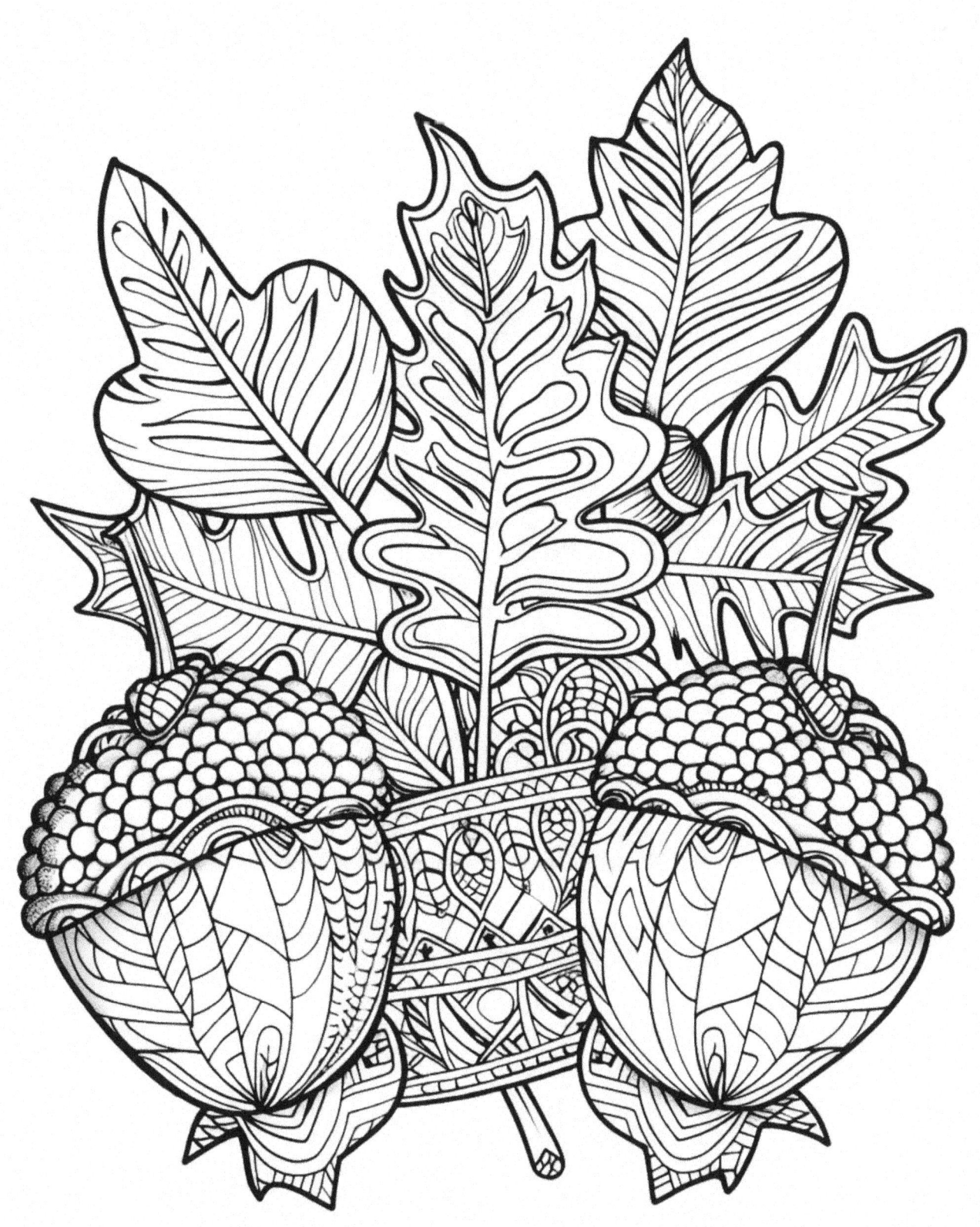

About the Developer

PleaseLetThemKnow, LLC is a small business that offers a wide range of books suitable for all age groups. Our product line includes medium, low-, and original works, available on Amazon's Kindle Book Publishing service. Our founder, Gary R. Brown, a retired U.S. Navy member, started this business in March 2023 to offer books, games, journals, and puzzle books for both children and seniors. We follow a cost-saving structure that benefits everyone and ensures our prices remain affordable.

At PleaseLetThemKnow, we believe in expanding our reach to bring our books to larger populations and areas. We always seek partners who share our vision and can help us achieve our goals. You can visit our website at www.pleaseletthemknow.com for more information and to explore our collection. Thank you for supporting our small business!

If you want to learn more about my creations, please visit my website at www.pleaseletthemknow.com. Additionally, I use Midjourney to enhance the visual appeal of my book and the Grammarly app to improve the quality of my writing. Midjourney helps me enhance my images, and the Grammarly app helps me check my grammar, spelling, and punctuation. These tools enable me to focus on creative writing while ensuring that the technical aspects of my work are also taken care of. We are committed to providing high-quality products at reasonable prices. I appreciate your support!

www.ingramcontent.com/pod-product-compliance
Lightning Source LLC
Chambersburg PA
CBHW081459040426
42446CB00016B/3308